Fire fighter

A fire fighter puts out fires and rescues people.

hose

helmet

boots

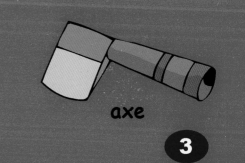

axe

3

Sailor

A sailor works
on a ship.

life boat

morse code machine

life jacket

telescope

Builder

A builder makes houses.

sand

hard hat

bricks

cement

7

Police officer

A police officer
catches criminals.

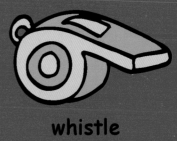

whistle

helmet

car

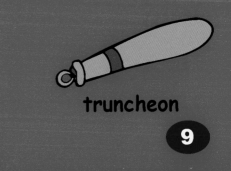

truncheon

9

Pilot

A pilot flies an aeroplane.

compass

aeroplane

radar

radio

11

Postman

A postman delivers letters to your house.

post sack

bicycle

stamps

uniform

13

Archaeologist

Archaeologists study the past.

magnifying glass

special brushes

metal detector

spade

Zoo keeper

A zoo keeper looks after animals.

keys

broom

water hose

shovel

17

Astronaut

An astronaut goes into space.

space suit

radio

computer

rocket

Road sweeper

A road sweeper keeps the roads clean.

gloves

bin

bin bags

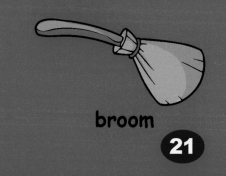

broom

Gardener

A gardener plants flowers.

seeds

spade

fork

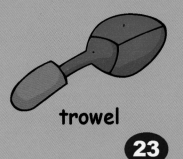
trowel

23

Lumberjack

A lumberjack cuts down trees.

goggles

safety harness

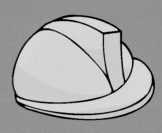

hard hat

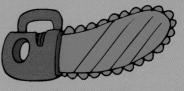

chainsaw